The Power of Collaboration
In Business

Bringing Everyone Together Series

business
Over Coffee

Published by Business Over Coffee International (BOCI)

Memphis, TN

Published by:

Business Over Coffee International (BOCI)
5865 Ridgeway Center Parkway Suite 300
Memphis, TN 38120

2nd Edition

Designed by: Sherri Henley

Cover Photography by: Caroline Norwood Wells

Formatted by: Delmar Johnson

Edited by: Joanne Derstine (1st edition), Carly Crawford (2nd edition)

Printed in the United States of America

DEDICATION

I personally dedicate this book to Team BOCI who brought this idea to fruition by understanding and modeling the power of collaboration in business. Thank you for your tenacious ability to build your professional presence while complementing another's ambition... multiplying your strength with the purpose of enlarging your territory with like-minded individuals. - Sherri Henley

ACKNOWLEDGEMENTS

To my family for encouraging me to spread my wings and fly toward creativity through long hours of poring over social media intelligence, collaborative opportunities and the personal evolution of digging deep to find answers from within.

To Delmar Johnson for showing up at the first "Business Over Coffee" event when there was an audience of 8 and no "I" on "BOC!" For listening and participating on BOCI Talk Radio when there were fewer than 30 listens per month. For affording us her expertise by formatting this book and assisting in the publishing process from beginning to end. Thank you, Delmar, for being a professional...as a business owner, BOCI Advisor and Founding Member.

To Caroline Norwood for expressing her artistic nature through photography. Thank you for gifting us with the business photo (final chapter) taken at BOCI Headquarters by CN Photography.

To Charlisha Renata Photography for investing collaborative time to provide professional photos for me. Your work speaks for itself!

To Virginia Rowland of Ridgeway Business Center (BOCI headquarters) for seeing the potential of a tiny seed and collaborating to build an international powerhouse!

To each author who contributed her intellectual property to add value to this book. Each of you is an amazing leader, mentor and professional. Thank you for being a fellow traveler on this journey.

To BOCI members who have watched us grow by leaps and bounds...and participated in the process.

To BOCI Executive Council and Advisors for your wealth of knowledge.

To BOCI Team Leaders, Consultants and Liaisons for your dedication to excellence.

CONTENTS

INTRODUCTION

THE POWER OF COLLABORATION IN BUSINESS
By Sherri Henley

There is strength in unity. For collaboration between select parties to become powerful in business, however, each player must uphold a similar value system or, given time, the collaboration is destined for failure. Partnering in name only defeats the intended purpose of joining hands to develop a larger powerhouse made of two or more entities linked as one. Linking online is only one aspect of a joint effort. *Behind the scenes meetings, body language,confidentiality, attitude and other behaviors that build strong relationships are where true commitment to integrity in business is met or denied.*

How Do We Size Up Connections as Collaborators?

I like to call a connection a soft collaboration - a partnership requiring *little effort.* For example, someone recently approached me about an idea. Ideas are great! Follow-through is another thing altogether. To determine whether this person was serious about his creative aspirations, I invited him to an event to talk afterward. Guess what. He showed up! We are still in negotiations, which could take weeks, months or even years...but the bricks are being laid. *When you lay one brick at a time, you are able to assess the foundation on a "lay as you go" basis. Instead of diving in deep I suggest wading in slowly.*

Create Accountability

A written agreement is as easy as an email. Once negotiations are completed, get it in writing! Recently, while sitting in a meeting with a high-ranking banker, we were discussing the importance of following regulations. He said, "I call email *evidence* mail." Remember...evidence can and will be used against you...or for you. Keep your end of the bargain and hold your partner's feet to the fire.

Renegotiate From Time to Time

Be quick to act upon a renegotiation if you believe you are unable to follow through, or if the collaborative side becomes yesterday's baggage due to lack of commitment. Remember that dynamics evolve with time; change is constant. It is important to revisit the table periodically to confirm that you are still on the same page as your partner.

Earn Respect, Demand Loyalty

Earning respect is a process that only time and experience will decide. Loyalty, however, should be expected of hand holders. When respect and loyalty meet, there is a match made in heaven, as neither can be bought nor sold. You must earn respect and demand loyalty to support the power of collaboration in business.

Learn From the Best

In the following pages, you will find a collection of Collaborative Authors who exhibit high standards of integrity, expertise and stability in business. They understand and model the correct intent of joining hands to accomplish a common goal: creating a winning solution for all involved. It is my distinct pleasure to bring everyone together, providing a prime example of leadership at its best.

Learn from these sought-after professionals, who share their individual stories mixed with their wealth of knowledge, and incorporate their expertise into your own success story.

SHERRI HENLEY, Founder and CEO, BOCI

Sherri Henley is *Bringing Everyone Together* through connections, collaboration, exposure and business.

As Founder and CEO of Business Over Coffee International (BOCI), author, speaker, social media intelligence trainer and collaborative leader, Sherri has learned the art of balancing life between being a wife, a mother of two small children and a community leader. In addition to effectively managing one of the Mid-South's fastest growing business networks with global reach, Sherri hosts weekly radio and television shows on BOCI Talk Radio Channel, BOCI TV and Sharing with Sherri. She also serves as local chapter board member of National Association of Women Business Owners (NAWBO). Recently quoted in *50 Seeds of Greatness,* authored by Germaine Moody – Sherri is a collaborative leader by example.

In addition to business success, Sherri is a published author of poetry, a recording artist and has served as pastor and president of non-profit organizations. Sherri presently serves as the program director for BOCI's Professional Boost Internship Program that highlights her initiative to invest into the lives of people with business aspirations. Sherri has also been recognized for her community efforts with awards including the Kindle Award by The Loretta McNary Show, Excellence Award by National College of Business and Technology, Outstanding Community Service Award by Networking in Memphis, Certificate of Appreciation by Girls

Inc. in recognition of facilitating leadership techniques based on Careers and Entrepreneurship, and Good Samaritan Award by International Fellowship of Pastoral Counselors and Chaplains.

Although Sherri remains in demand, her demeanor remains one of humble beginnings. Raised in a pastor's home, Sherri's beliefs and actions are based upon core Christian values.These values are the basis of the integrity upheld by the executive council and advisors of BOCI, and embrace the life mission of Sherri Henley...Bringing Everyone Together.

Visit: www.businessovercoffee.com,www.sherrihenley.com

CHAPTER ONE

ARE YOU THE "I" OR "WE" IN TEAM?
By Sherri Henley

You may be thinking...there is no "I" *nor* "We" in TEAM! You are correct...in terms of spelling. But in *Territorial Mentality*, think again.

Consider the Ego of People

The "I" in teamis often obvious within the ranks of officials, politicians, family members, community and church. It's more about "me" than "we," thus the *cause and effect* of what I call *The Trust Factor Decline.*

A Wise Man Once Said...

"Begin your sentences with 'We' when speaking with (not to) your team."

By applying this advice I have been afforded the opportunity to lead many teams to grow with respect for one another while adopting the *"We've Got Your Back!"* attitude.

If you need to guard your back...you are either on the wrong team or you are the "I" who should convert to the "We" vernacular.

Ask Yourself These Questions...

1. *Would I want to be trapped in a foxhole with a teammate who thinks like me?*

2. *Would I want my colleagues to overhear my unspoken intentions?*

If you answered *yes,* then*congratulations! You are part of the "We" in TEAM*. Otherwise, you are a weak link; transform your thinking in order to uphold the goals of the unit as a whole.

How Do I Transform My Thinking?

Your mindset is embedded in your being. You must input specific code (out with the old...in with the new) to transform your thinking into positive behavior that becomes contagious. We find contagious behavior exhibited on both sides of the coin — positive *and* negative. Encourage positivity by modeling the upbeat behavior you desire on your team.

Begin Changing Your Mind

Begin changing your mind by reading books by *authors* you respect, recommended by *people* you respect. I highly recommend authors Bob Burg, Shelley Baur, Loretta McNary, Ed Horrell and Ivan Misner, to name a few excellent resources for professional and personal development.

Time to Check Yourself!

Take Introspective Inventory of How Well You are
Operating as a Team Player:

1. *Do I consider the other person?*

2. *Do I listen to concerns of the team even when I offer a different opinion?*

3. *How well am I connecting with teammates?*

4. *Do I view change as an opportunity to evolve?*

SHELLEY PAGE BAUR

President, Integrity-Based Communications

After a career that ranged from field sales to Vice President-Communications in corporate America, Shelley Page Baur wrote *Integrity-Based Communications:Using Truth to Get What You **Really** Want (2004).* She continues to teach the six principles that transform people and build high-trust relationships, and has a fascination for integrating and aligning internal learning expertise with external communications.

Shelley is a graduate of the University of Memphis (BA, Psychology), founding member and past president of the National Association of Women Business Owners (NAWBO) and graduate and past board member of Leadership Memphis (program chair 2006-2008). She remains active with Business Network International, Business Over Coffee International, American Society for Training and Development, Society for Human Resource Management (SHRM) ethics council and currently serves in mentoring/advisory roles with the University of Memphis MILE leadership program.

Shelley has been honored by **Memphis Woman** magazine as one of "Fifty Women Who Make a Difference" and is an Athena Award recipient as a role model for mentoring and community leadership, IRIS Award winner for encouraging women entrepreneurs, and Leadership Memphis Distinguished Alumnus Award.

Active as a speaker and trainer/coach, Shelley is passionate about building people for life and leadership based on her Integrity-Based Communications leadership model and new book, ***Integrity-Based Communications:****Using Truth To Build High-Trust Relationships.*

Visit: www.shelleybaur.com,
www.integritybasedcommunications.com

CHAPTER TWO

BEGIN WITH "WE"
By Shelley Page Baur

When Sherri Henley and I first talked about this book project, my mind traveled back in time to many experiences and many ways Ilearned that "we" is more powerful than "I."

One key point I shared with Sherri was how I came to believe that there is no lack of supply in the universe. Our world was created for us to live abundantly. Despite what the media wants to us to believe – or past business philosophies that were poured into our minds – we need not fear lossor competition. The way to success is through collaboration, creating win-win solutions for all parties involved.

Beginning With Values

Among the first things we agreed upon – and totally respected about one another – was allowing our integrity to govern everything we do personally and professionally. That value became the basis for our relationship, and we acknowledged that it would govern the like-minded people we would attract into our mutual space.

We applied this principle specifically in the area of membership in two business networking organizations: Business Over Coffee International (BOCI), with 1,000+ members in less than two years, founded by Sherri Henley, and Business Network International (BNI), with 145,000 members in 28 years, founded by Ivan Misner. Some members (of each organization) were confused about the distinction of the organizations' offerings, and clearly concerned about crossing the line or "breaking the rules."

Today, Sherri and I are each members of both organizations, regularly working collaboratively on events and cross-promotion. At the outset, we thought it necessary to talk through the ways the two organizations were *alike*. Commonalities included the following:

1. Live networking events
2. Educational opportunities
3. Making and deepening relationships to influence business
4. Business profiles, encouraged for online promotion, free of charge.

Then we compared the ways the two organizations were *different*.

BOCI is:

- Informal, "come and go" as schedule allows
- Internet streamed for real-time virtual attendance at a majority of live events
- Recorded for future access
- Promoted heavily through social media, with optional monthly training
- No structured expectation for referrals
- Open membership, with possible multiple competitors sharing the same space
- Founded and owned by Sherri Henley, advised by volunteer executive council and advisory, with chapter partnerships available
- Annual BOCI *virtual membership* is free of charge, including online professional profile.
- Annual BOCI *professional membership* is $100 per year, and includes annual BOCI-TV interview, BOCI Talk Radio interview, BOCI weekly events (four per month; 48-50 per year), and multiple business reviews for social media, presentation skills, website analysis, image consulting and more.

BNI emphasizes:

- Adherence to policies, procedures, and publicly-pledged code of ethics
- One-to-one meetings with chapter members to learn more about each others' businesses and marketing strategies
- Adherence to 90-minute meeting agenda (in chapters throughout the world)

- Mandatory training (minimum once per year, prior to renewal)

- Weekly accountability for attendance (or qualified substitute)
- Weekly accountability for referral follow-up
- Referral-based business introductions
- Tracking dollar value for business referred, translatable into membership financial return on investment
- Category exclusivity, having only one member per niche category, based on written application and leadership acceptance
- BNI is a franchise, with global guidelines for compliance by local Directors.

- Annual BNI membership is $365, plus local chapter dues, if applicable.

Because of tracking numbers, we know that in 2012:

- BNI was the largest business networking organization in the world.
- BNI had 145,000 members worldwide,
- BNI generated 7.1 million referrals resulting in $3.3 billion worth of business for its members.

Making an Informed Decision Makes Sense

With these details in mind, Sherri Henley and Jana Cardona (area BNI executive director/franchisee) met and agreed that the respective business models could thrive side by side.

As previously stated, some members of each organization expressed initial confusion about the distinction of the organizations' offerings, and were clearly concerned about crossing the line or "breaking the rules." But quite comfortably, and for many different reasons, many people now are members of both organizations. Since reasons for joining are different for each person, the ability to clearly explain the differences between the two groups melts away the fear of competition.

Moving beyond this example of collaboration between two highly respected organizations, I regularly encourage like-minded people to meet, get to know one another, and learn each other's values, strengths, preferences and ideal clientele. Oftentimes, people working under the same umbrella (communications, for instance) find themselves using the same strategies to attract business (e.g. professional speaking for a fee, an intentional showcase pro bono), but each of them considers his most desired client or preferred assignment to be quite different from the other's – even though both may possess the broader competency (e.g. communications related to social media marketing vs. presentation skills training paired with personal coaching). If a bid proposal needs deeper bench strength and more capacity than one company can deliver, competitors should vet one another before tackling a joint venture or partnership to land the deal. Not surprisingly, the more lead time, the better.

Recently, I spoke to members of the National Association of Women Business Owners (NAWBO) about this very subject. I began with sharing the communication model outlined in the 2013 edition of my book, ***Integrity-Based Communications***: *Using Truth To Build High-Trust Relationships*[3].

Bob Burg, author of *Endless Referrals*[4], says, "People do business with – and refer business to – people they know, like and trust." The six behaviors of Integrity-Based Communications (IBC)[3] are a model to accomplish that very goal in business and beyond, by developing high-trust relationships regardless of the situation or application. Used consistently, IBC is a tool that creates honest, authentic conversations through direct, respectful exchange, encouraging like-minded people to go deeper and relate better to one another.

1. Tell your truth quicker, faster
2. Ask for what you want

Acknowledging that people do things for their reasons, not ours, be diligent in uncovering what motivates, drives and rewards others, and "makes another person's heart sing." It may be that your seemingly identical niche is, in fact, quite different.

3. Ask questions
4. Pay attention to learn what will drive a win-win outcome

When people discover that we really do what we *say* we will do – and give the courtesy of re-negotiating our agreements as soon as we realize we cannot deliver as agreed – we build credibility with one another. These are the people who take personal responsibility, which extends to all areas of their lives. These are the people who do not make excuses or blame others, but own up to the consequences of the choices they have made. These are the high-trust relationships we treasure. These are the people with whom we want to do business. This is the way we want to be seen. Mutually, we stake our reputations on these behaviors.

     5. Keep your agreements

     6. Give and receive accountability

Business Owners: Specialize

Using the IBC model provided, I encourage business owners to seriously reflect upon where their own "sweet spot" is...where their skill, passion, and buying marketplace overlap. This is where I recommend that people **specialize.** Specialization will allow them to do what makes their heart sing and to make the greatest impact in serving others.

PRODUCTIVITY PROCESS ALIGNMENT TOOL

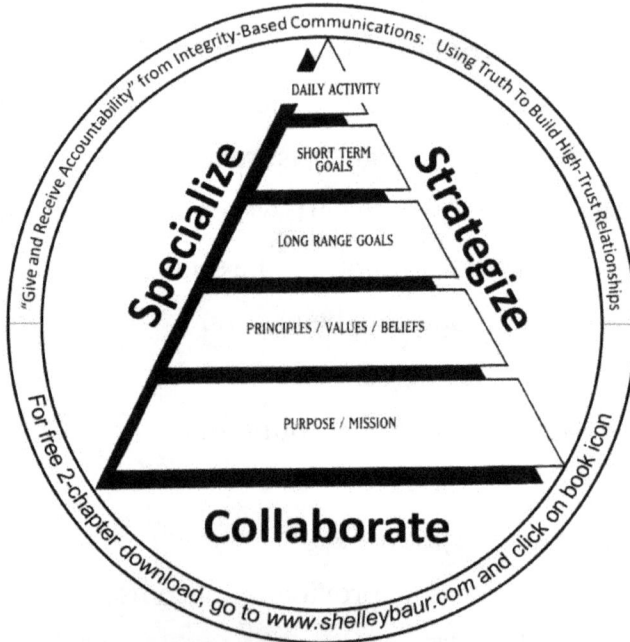

"Give and Receive Accountability" from Integrity-Based Communications: Using Truth To Build High-Trust Relationships

For free 2-chapter download, go to www.shelleybaur.com and click on book icon

Specialize

Strategize

DAILY ACTIVITY

SHORT TERM GOALS

LONG RANGE GOALS

PRINCIPLES / VALUES / BELIEFS

PURPOSE / MISSION

Collaborate

Since answering Brian Tracy's question, "What would you do if you knew you could not fail?"[5] in 1994, I have known that I would write a book that would change people's lives for the better. In 2004, that book, *Integrity-Based Communications[3]*, was first published. This is my core message as a keynote speaker, and this is the foundational

module for every training program I develop and deliver –
from client engagement, to presentation skills coaching, to
sustainability, to diversity/inclusion, and to teambuilding.

During that time, I learned that building people for life
and leadership was my passion, and I became a student of the
best leaders in the leadership talent development industry:
Brian Tracy, Stephen Covey, Don Hutson, Patricia Fripp, Ed
Champagne, Deepak Chopra, Wayne Dyer, Bonnie Taylor, and
Mark Victor Hansen. I also studied the curricula of
Development Dimensions International (DDI)[6], Wilson
Learning,[7] and the Kauffman Foundation[8].

Today, I have fine-tuned my niche. Teaching Integrity-
Based Communications[3] is where I have chosen to specialize.
For clients who hire me, I make a point to add more value – at
no additional charge – by offering marketing advice and
counsel where I believe it can make an impact or improve an
outcome.

Strategize

After careful analysis of your organization, take a look at
those people and organizations you see as competitors. Now
consider them, instead, as potential partners for strategic

alliances, joint ventures, or simply working together on a project. Where is the best fit? What would the project management look like? How will you approach them? What does the opportunity look like in the short term? Long-term? What are the best possible opportunities? Obstacles? What would a proposed win-win look like?

Collaborate

For me, the best alliances have been with past clients, a business coach, a curriculum development expert, an internet marketing guru, other authors, speakers, and trainers whose expertise complements mine. In each case, we are strengthened by one another. More importantly, however, our solution offering is more robust, better serving our clients.

Discussion and agreement should be focused on these and other topics:

- How business is invoiced, including who issues 1099s to independent contractors
- Insurance coverage to protect all entities
- Who gets what share of compensation, project by project

- Details related to every step of client engagement through execution
- How the client is shared after the partnership is ended
- Legal counsel for contracts – keep it as simple as possible

The point is this: ***cooperation and collaboration trump competition any day of the week...especially when it is accomplished in the pursuit of serving a higher goal.*** That philosophy has helped me grow my business steadily and successfully, affirming that the foundation for building a high-trust business is based on first having high-trust relationships.

With due diligence and thoughtful consideration, venture into the process of looking at your own special niche. You will discover that your "sweet spot" is usually where the great joy in serving is to be found. Have you already found what makes your heart sing? Can it be monetized in today's marketplace? If yes, that is where you should specialize!

Strategize about the best possible partnerships that complement yours. Make a list of the most obvious people, and begin the conversation.

I encourage and celebrate your collaborative success, beginning each sentence with "we." Begin the thoughtful, intentional process of building people – and a business – and enjoy the reality: *"We are stronger together."*

NOTES

[1] Business Over Coffee International (BOCI), http://businessovercoffee.com

[2] Business Network International (BNI), *http://bni.com*

[3] Shelley Page Baur, **Integrity-Based Communications: Using truth to get what you *really* want** (2004), **Integrity-Based Communications: Using Truth To Build High-Trust Relationships** (2013).

[4] Bob Burg, **Endless Referrals**, McGraw-Hill Companies, 1994.

[5] Brian Tracy, **The Phoenix Seminar for Maximum Achievement**, http://tracyint.com/index.php.89.html

[6] http://www.ddiworld.com

[7] http://wilsonlearning.com

[8] *www.kauffman.org*

JANA CARDONA

Executive Director for BNI (Business Network International) in west Tennessee and North Mississippi. There are currently 18 BNI chapters in the Mid-South region, with around 460 members. Conservatively, these chapters generated around $14 million in income in 2012.

Jana is also a networking and referral marketing speaker, coach and trainer. Her passion is helping individuals and companies develop a solid marketing strategy that enables them to do business by referral. She has a keen ability to listen as a person explains what he does and who he is looking for, and then perceives what key elements are missing. Teaching them how to clarify and rephrase to receive quality referrals is her goal.

Jana is married and has two grown children and six grandchildren. Her favorite pastimes are studying personal development, playing with her grandchildren and enjoying nature.

Visit: www.janacardona.com, www.bnimidsouth.com

CHAPTER 3

COLLABORATION IS THE NEW COMPETITION

By Jana Cardona

Competition is a familiar word in business. As a sales associate or business owner,you typically want to gain the edge over your competitor. Yet more and more we are seeing and hearing the phrase "collaboration is the new competition." The movement today is away from *competition* and toward *cooperation* and *harmony*. Instead of going solo or being a one man show, the shift now is toward *teamwork*.

Why should we build a team? Simple - because today's challenges are often more than any one person can do alone. Successful teamwork is built on collaboration. Does your team just include people from your company, or can it include *competitors?*

Do you think more as a collaborator or as a competitor? Do you have to be one or the other? Can you be both?

Most are familiar with the definition of competition. But some may not be as familiar with the word collaboration.

Collaboration: Working with one another to do a task. It is a recurring process where two or more people or organizations work together to realize shared goals; a deep, collective, determination to reach an identical objective.

Why would you choose to collaborate? There is one main reason:to serve your customer by delivering the best product or service. The question is whether you and/or your company is able to provide *everything* your client needs *all the time* to deliver the best product or service. When we examine many of today's businesses, we see a multitude of "one stop shops." Companies have expanded into multiple divisions or branches in an effort to keep the client totally under one roof--theirs! Hence, a multitude of businesses overlap in services. When other companies carry some of our same products or services, we may choose to view them as our direct competition.

Stumbling Blocks to Collaboration

Is it true that competitors can't work together? Or are there possibilities for incorporating collaboration? In too many cases, there are perceived stumbling blocks that impede collaboration. We will examine two in this chapter.

In my role as BNI (Business Network International) Executive Director and a networking speaker, coach and trainer, I often hear professionals sweep a very broad brush over their explanation when asked the question, "So, what do you do?" Phrases such as, "I can do everything" or "We can handle all your needs" are expected to clearly define their services. Yet, they do just the opposite.

When you present yourself as a generalist, no one is sure what you can do *well*. Do you have a specialty or strong suit? When that is unclear, one might conclude, "Since I know no one can do *everything* extremely well, I wonder if their work is going to deliver the quality I need."

If you have a specific problem to solve, or a need to fill, would you have more confidence in a generalist or a specialist? For example, if you had a brain tumor, would you trust a general practitioner to operate? No, you would certainly rather have a brain surgeon (a specialist) operate. Carrying the medical analogy further, when we are in the hospital, we know that several different doctors will be consulted, one for each specific area of the body that needs attention.

Let's examine a second stumbling block. It is the feeling that if you admit there is an area where another company can do a better job for the client, you risk losing the client entirely by handing him over to the other company or person to complete that phase of the project. This is a genuine fear, particularly if you don't really know or trust the competitor.

Now let's take these two stumbling blocks and see if we can design a way to incorporate collaboration.

Teaming Up for Superb Service

The first step is to evaluate your areas of expertise. What do you and/or your company do 70% of the time? What is your passion, the area where you really shine? What can you do, but would rather not take the time to do because either it is more trouble than it is worth, or it is just not your "thing." You *will* do it if you *have to,* butyou would rather not spend the time. What if the 30% you *could* do, but would rather not do, or an area that is not really a passion, can be done by someone else – a collaborative partner?

Visualize a client you have just counseled in your office. You've analyzed his needs and you know that, generally speaking, you and your company can fill most, if not all, of those needs. Yet, if you are totally honest, while you can provide excellent service for *most* of those needs, there are a few areas where the product or quality of service you and your company provides is *only adequate.* The project would turn out great in most areas, but a little weaker in others.

You have a dilemma. In the old mode of thinking, you

don't want to lose your client to a competitor. Yet, you know in your heart that the competitor really does have a superior product or service for that particular aspect of your client's needs.

Bill Cates, in his book *Unlimited Referrals,* relates the following story.

"In the mid-1970s, John Mueller worked as a representative for the 3M Company. He sold film used in the printing process. He says, 'We lost the business to Kodak; our product did not perform. I not only removed our film, but I picked up the Kodak film, delivered it, and optimized it to minimize downtime. When our new product worked, we got the business back!'"

This is a tremendous example of putting the needs of the customer above your own.

Think about this paradigm shift. What if you purposely builtrelationships with several experts, albeit your competitors, who could deliver higher quality products and services in the areas of your company's *weaker* services.

The key here is that you *purposely build relationships* and know that you can *trust them* to help you serve, not steal, your clients. Now, when you collaborate, each of you provides that niche service needed to deliver a superb package to your client. This exemplifies the definition of collaboration.

I came across this quote by K.R. Sridhar, founder of Bloom Energy, a fuel cell company, which spoke volumes regarding this way of thinking: "When you obsess about the customer, you end up defeating your competition as a byproduct. When you are just obsessed about the competition, you end up killing yourself because you are not focused on the customer."

When we are honest with ourselves about where our areas of expertise lie, and where they do not, and then purposely develop relationships with professionals who can fill the gaps in our expertise, we fulfill the definition of collaboration -- two or more people or organizations working together to realize shared goals – and our customer is the winner!

Collaboration is the key!

JO GARNER

Founder, Talk Shoppe

Jo Garner is a mortgage officer with extensive knowledge in tailoring mortgages to her customers who are refinancing or purchasing homes throughout the country. She offers conventional, FHA, VA or other loan programs for refinancing and purchases. Jo can help you look at rent vs. buy, when it makes sense to refinance, and how to get the best deal on your home purchasefinancing.

Jo Garner has been in the real estate/financing business for over 20 years. She got her start in Portland, Maine where she first began her real estate career. She received her real estate education from the University of Southern Maine and was personally mentored in San Diego, California, by Robert G. Allen, author of *Nothing Down,Creating Wealth* and <u>The Challenge.</u>

After moving back to West Tennessee in 1987, she went into business buying and selling discounted owner-financed notes secured on real estate. In 1990, Jo went to work for a residential mortgage company and has been a mortgage loan officer for over 17 years. Her goal is to offer excellent, affordable service to her customers, tailoring the loan programs to the specific needs of her clients.

In addition to her work in the mortgage field, Jo Garner is the primary sponsor and founder of Talk Shoppe in Memphis. Jo also hosts the Real Estate Mortgage Shoppe program on News Radio 600 WREC and iHEART Radio.

For past podcasts and other blog posts,
visit: www.MortgageLoansBlog.com , www.talkshoppe.biz

Also visit: www.MoneyShoppe.NET, jogarner@mindspring.com

CHAPTER 4

EXPAND YOUR SPHERE OF INFLUENCE
By Jo Garner

We all have success stories of times when we joined our talents and resources with other people to bring about exponential results. Andrew Carnegie was wise in his definition of the word "collaboration." He said "Teamwork... is the fuel that allows common people to attain uncommon results."

You may remember the story of "The Bundle of Sticks" from Aesop's fables. A mother had six strong sons who thought they could do everything, each using his own effort. They kept trying and failing at the assignments they were given to accomplish.

One day the mother handed one of her sons a bundle of sticks and asked him to break it for firewood. He tried and tried but could not break the bundle of sticks. Mama took the bundle away and handed it to another son who also could not break the bundle of sticks.

Finally Mama, a little exasperated, took the bundle, untied the string holding the sticks together, and handed each son a stick. This time when she asked them to break the bundle, they each broke the one stick they were holding in their hands. When each handed his broken stick back to his mother, the whole bundle had been broken at the same time because each son broke his one stick. In a matter of seconds, the whole bundle of sticks was broken because Mama's sons used a form of collaboration called "teamwork."

Like this mother's sons, Talk Shoppe, Business Over Coffee International(BOCI) and other networking groups have come together to share their knowledge, resources and marketing to help each group experience uncommon, exponential results. Talk Shoppe has always encouraged our participants to get actively involved with at least three dedicated groups. The person positively engaged with three other organizations — like a business club, a church group or networking group — tends to be more valuable to these groups where he belongs because of his expanding sphere of influence.

Talk Shoppe offers free education and networking to anyone interested in business or real estate. The group meets every Wednesday 9A-10A CST at DeVry University, 6401 Poplar Ave 6th floor in Memphis, TN 38119. Each week, we have an educational speaker which we film and post on the internet at www.TalkShoppe.BIZ when the presentation is completed. Some weeks, we offer a group participation event. About eight times a year, Talk Shoppe presents the Mastermind Principle, based on *Think and Grow Rich* by Napoleon Hill, where business people break into groups of no more than four and share and receive ideas, resources and referrals with the other business people in their group.

Depending on the number in the audience, Talk Shoppe invites each person attending the event to stand up and share with the audience who they are, their business name, and contact information or referral request. We play a short networking game called Talk Shoppe Tag to help get people in the room connected with each other. The beginning and end of our Talk Shoppe sessions are made available for freestyle networking.

For Talk Shoppe's advertisers, sponsors and speakers, we offer a variety of media platforms for promoting themselves and their businesses. We are one of the few groups who regularly distribute printed fliers around the city announcing our events and promoting our paying advertisers. We offer social media promotions once a month and short radio promotions on the air on News Radio AM 600 WREC and iHEART Radio. We also invite our advertisers and speakers to join us the third week of the month an hour before Talk Shoppe to our lead-generating Think Tank meeting where we share our resources with other advertisers in our group.

Talk Shoppe participants frequently share success stories. Many of these stories involve various types of collaboration and networking practices. The keys to these success stories seem to repeat common denominators. Those common denominators involve practicing the principle of "givers gain," introduced by Business Network International (BNI) founder Ivan Misner, and regular follow-up with people within the networking organization.

Lance and Terri Walker of Walker Auctions willingly share their talents each year raising millions of dollars for charitable causes. After doing a magnificent job raising money at Talk Shoppe to helpfund a **Make-A-Wish** surprise for a child, the Walkers received not one, but two estate auction jobs. They have received much repeat business from loyal referring partners due to their practice of "givers gain."

So many of our sponsors and advertisers have gotten business leads, not just from our own social media posts about ourselves, but from positive posts from other members of our Talk Shoppe Think Tank advertising group. Repeated, third-party endorsements on various social media sites can reach exponentially more people than just the members of your own sphere of influence. The more your audience sees you and your business, the more often you come to the front of their minds when they come across someone needing your product or service.

Three aspects that distinguish Talk Shoppe from other groups are:

1. The Talk Shoppe events are free to the public. We are supported by our advertisers.

2. We place a high priority on education as well as networking activities.

3. We do not hamper our participants with rules and regulations about attendance and mandatory referrals within the group. However, we do encourage our participants to refer within the group when they have an opportunity to do so.

"Givers gain" is a proven concept. We allow non-profit groups a free table sponsorship at our events to promote their causes and ask for support from our audience.

Continually following up with people in your target market and in your networking spheres creates more opportunities for people to refer business to you. You can find Talk Shoppe and our participants regularly on Facebook at www.facebook.com/talkshoppememphis, our website www.TalkShoppe.BIZ, and on the radio every Tuesday 9:30AM -10:00AM CST on the Talk Shoppe Show aired live on BOCI Talk Radio Channel.

CAROLYN BENDALL

Owner and President, Fashion Academy

President of **Fashion Academy**, Carolyn is a Master Colour Analysis Consultant and Total Image Consultant with many practical years of experience using and perfecting the Fashion Academy and Your True Colours curriculum and skin undertone system. As owner and president of Fashion Academy, the school, its products and skin undertone system, Carolyn has worked feverishly to ensure that her consultants are positioned to penetrate all aspects of the fashion industry around the United States. Training countless numbers of consultants and educating thousands of people to the revolutionary idea that the consumer does have the power to stop the madness of fads and impractical designs in their daily lives, Carolyn's presentations draw smiles of approbation wherever she expounds her cause, be it on television, in trade shows or in presentations. Her exuberance is refreshing, and her promotion of the Fashion Academy principles and purpose elicits positive feedback wherever she goes. Her fierce devotion to the end consumer drives Carolyn's resolve to demand a product base and service that takes into consideration the customer's individuality and lifestyle. To find a voice for all ages and needs in the fashion world is Carolyn's lifetime quest, and under her leadership, Fashion Academy, its instructors and its graduates are becoming a powerful voice for the betterment of the fashion retail industry.

Carolyn has been an ardent supporter and educator to the backbone of the fashion industry, the men and women who day after day serve the end consumer with their fashion needs: hair stylists, color consultants, dressmakers, tailors, permanent makeup technicians and sales people in all areas of fashion retail. In her opinion, these are the experts who may have a good idea what consumers need and want but are often faced with the dilemma of how best to serve their clients' interests, especially when fads dictate otherwise. The Fashion Academy colour determining system provides credibility to the consultant's diagnosis, thus enhancing customer satisfaction, and ensuring repeat business.

Visit: www.fashionacademy.biz

CHAPTER 5

BRAND YOURSELF AS AN EXPERT
By Carolyn Bendall

Many of us who start a business are on a shoestring budget, and making every dollar work for the betterment of the company is at the top of the list. However, choosing to be our own marketing directors out of necessity sometimes places us in a difficult position. We know our business, but we're not sure how to promote it effectively.

For marketing, sometimes the dollar value has to be placed on you, the marketer and networker. It is your business - your dream - that you are making happen and no one else has the passion for what you believe in better than you. You can make that passion work for you when you don't have the budget to hire someone else.

We purchased Fashion Academy almost on a whim, and therefore with no allocated monies. Prior to purchasing the business, I had worked on my own as an independent Image Consultant trained by Fashion Academy. In an effort to promote myself, I had sent out many, many letters, but received nothing from this direct mail tactic. I had to find other unique ways to be noticed.

How I Marketed Myself

The first step I took was to attend a Continuing Education Class on Fashion at the University of Memphis, to see thecompetition. The class assured me that my training far exceeded what was required to represent this subject best. By the end of the week, I had an entire presentation put together and an appointment with the Continuing Education Department. They loved what we had and put us on the next semester's schedule, right up against the other class that I attended. The following semester, the other class was dropped from the offerings.

The next step I pursued was to associate my name as the expert in the region, utilizing a friendship with a designer who knew the editor of *Women's News of the Mid-South*. My friend mentioned to the editor that I would be contacting her, so when I sent her my email with my proposal of writing a Question and Answer column each month on image, in exchange for a byline with my contact info, she was ready with her response. She agreed it was something that was needed in the periodical.

I had set a goal for myself. When I could get FedEx (the major company headquartered in Memphis) to answer my letters and book me for a seminar, I would know I had "made it." Through the University of Memphis Continuing Education catalog, companies would contact those instructors that taught subjects they needed. FedEx called me before I ever sent them a letter!

I needed some webpage experience to eventually place myself on the internet, so I volunteered to work on a family-based web page. I noticed that one of the contributors was from Memphis, and that she worked with fragrance and cosmetics. We met for lunch and I showed her what I did. She decided that I needed to have fragrance cards and testers at all my seminars. That was the beginning of a wonderful relationship with Oscar de la Renta, which eventually led to my being invited to dinner with the sales associates and none other than Oscar de la Renta.

Because of the articles in *Memphis Woman* (the name had changed by this time), I met and developed a relationship with Barbara Bradley, the fashion editor of the *Commercial Appeal*, the Mid-South newspaper. After seeing our system, she wrote an article about me, which kept me in appointments for up to two years. When we purchased Fashion Academy, Barbara was the first one I told, and she wrote another story about our purchasing the company and bringing it to Memphis.

As I stood in the booth for *Memphis Woman,* the editor, Lisa Montgomery, and I listened to the person for fashion that the Southern Women's Show had booked. Lisa introduced me to the director of the show and told them that I needed to be on stage the next year. That began a wonderful relationship with the Southern Women's Show, which has provided us a booth at no monetary cost. In turn, I have worked many hours for them.

Networking Builds on Itself

Through the Southern Women's Show, I developed arelationship with Graceland, doing fashion show fundraisers with the Memphis Police Department. That connection enabled me to give a VIP visiting friend a quick tour of the famous mansion.

Always have your business card handy, and one that can be written on without smearing. Use the card to remind people what you talked about. I handed my business card to the *Essence* editor, with the name of the person they were to ask for when they got to Graceland.

Always be willing to give back. In fact, offer first; never be the one asking for the favor. "What can I do for you?" should be on your tongue and flow quickly and easily. But only offer if you are able and willing to actually work with them. If you can't — if it is beyond your capability — then let them know. Do not promise, then fail to deliver. (Granted, there will always be the emergency that comes up!)

It is still odd to me to hear people refer to me as a fashion expert, but I have worked hard to build that reputation. Our latest collaboration effort with Business Over Coffee International (BOCI) has introduced to me the wonders of the internet, and through utilizing my previous networking contacts, I have been able to help BOCI host influential guests. In turn, Sherri Henley, founder and CEO of BOCI, has offered me the opportunity to host Your True Colours Radio weekly, aired on BOCI Talk Radio Channel, and once a month I host BOCI TV, increasing my visibility and resume.

Always be willing to work and collaborate.

MARY SINGER, CCIM, CPM

Founder and CEO, CRG Sustainable Solutions

After 23 years of providing corporate real estate services that support clients' businesses, Ms. Singer continues to assist businesses with her leadership role in Corporate Sustainability. It is a new management philosophy of planning that balances the need for economic growth with environmental protection and social equality.

This deeper commitment to the new energy era supports her desire to help companies and communities make smarter choices to protect our natural resources. Reducing waste and inefficiency within an organization saves money and protects the environment.

Her partnering to advance sustainability with many experts includes:

- Sondra Wilson, as operations manager for 18+ years!
- Jill Schmitt, her daughter, who brings facility efficiencies to the forefront for corporations.
- Shelley Baur, who helps to communicate the sustainability story with integrity.
- Dr. Donald C. Fisher, who advances Global Reporting Initiative (GRI) and The Baldrige Criteria.
- Anthony Gilbreath, who has international experience in alternative energy, oil, gas and strategic sustainability.
- Dr. Shawn Jones, who has expertise in supply chain optimization, training and advisory skills.

- Greg Mitchell, who merges sustainability and strategy for lasting results.

CRG Sustainable Solutions specializes in sustainability analysis, planning and implementation to support organizations in their goals of achieving a triple bottom line. Twitter: @CRGss, Facebook: https://www.facebook.com/crgss

Visit: http://crgsustainablesolutions.com, www.wbecsouth.org, www.WBENC.org

CHAPTER 6

COLLABORATION + SUSTAINABILITY = "WE" IMPACT
By Mary Singer

By definition, collaboration means working together. When sustainability is added, the entity has capacity to endure. There has never been a better time to merge these strategies into impacts that can change how we use our natural resources of tomorrow.

My individual influence started within my family as an eight year old child. It seemed that collaboration + sustainability came very easy to me. Of course, I did not use those big sophisticated words. I used words with my family like, " I need help!," "How can we make this work?," or "There is no money to buy that!" A very ill mother and a family with limited income provided that first opportunity of common purpose, from sharing the chores to growing and preparing food to create a family performance for sustaining.

Grandparents, aunts and uncles taught us the importance of not being wasteful and how to leave the world a better place. It was this family value that became a part of how I live each day. That early journey created an embedded pathway: putting teams together (brothers, sister and adults) + common commitment (WE have to eat. WE must do chores) = performance (WE made it!).

How did this early childhood seed of collaboration +sustainabilty manifest in my adulthood life?

As a small business owner in the late 80s, I learned very quickly that owning a small,isolated business led to working extremely hard. The limitations created a drain on my time, wasted resources and disjointed activities. Collaboration lead me to go far beyond "me" to reach into larger markets to understand the WE. With a visionary agenda of reaching BIG, I soon realized the influence that WE teams could have on my business. Cresa, an international corporate real estate advisory firm, created a team of like minded commercial real estate service providers that this year just celebrated their 20th anniversary. I owe so much of my earlier career path to that BIG team of great men and women who came together. The value WE had together was huge. We:

- Communicated openly

- Shared ideas that could be broken down into smaller success stories

- Built trust

- Promoted independent thinking

- Shared a common commitment

Created HIGH PERFORMANCE.

Our time line looked something like this:

1985: Started a local Commercial Real Estate Firm that innovatively shook up the normal landlord model of leasing commercial real estate.

1990: WE turned the local platform into a national platform.

1995: WE turned the national platform into a global company.

2009: My daughter moved from mentorship to leadership in the organization that I founded in TN by reaching outside my market and collaborating with the BIG boys. She carries the WE commercial real estate story forward.

2010: I rebranded/recycled my original ideas around the facility footprint to create a new vision that included the environmental and social footprint....a grand purpose around saving natural resources. [1]

So here I am on this collaboration + sustainability =

WE impact path again. This time the WE part of the conversation is much larger than a business strategy. It includes reducing the use of resources and being efficient for profitability. The new team of WE includes small business owners that are providing services on a new playing field, such as tracking carbon emissions, reporting results into the CDP (Carbon Disclosure Project), adding integrity based training modules for the wisdom to do what is right for our resources, cutting waste in the supply chain and other creative partners. Today's message is all about our environment and how our businesses, communities and each of us individually are the WE connection with everything.

The collaboration strategy + sustainability = grand social WE purpose

When social media skills are overlaid onto a small business sustainability strategy, this advances the business agenda by casting a media net not only through the collaborating businesses but the communities to which they each are connected. Sustainability is all about being efficient by sharing knowledge and resources; what better way to connect with engaged people than to promote through the masses? Millions of conversations are occuring every day that help consumers make decisions, businesses to updateand networks and people to get things done.

Business Over Coffee International (BOCI)[2] is one of the perfect answers for a small business wanting to build relationships and advance a much bigger message socially than they could maintain individually. WE continue to find creative ways not only to promote what we are doing in business, but also ways to connect to businesses that want vibrant social connections in our community.

WE are experiencing progressive business leaders reframing their social presence from the grassroots all the way to the heart of the operation, in a way that engages businesses, their employees and their communities. Twitter, Facebook and YouTube are being used by big and small businesses to tell of their good deeds. The first social media sustainability index was published in 2011. It took large companies that reported into Dow Jones Sustainability Index and created an idex that follows how they use social media to influence sharing their good messages for saving resources. Small businesses can mimic this through BOCI's ability to provide social media tools, which help people connect on many levels via interactive technologies.[3]

Two amazing women, Anne Deeter and Amy Howell, just published *Women In High Gear*, which is all about integrating the world of social media into the marketing mix, enabling us to become worldwide media experts. One of the chapters in their book is titled "The Power of Communications: Whoever Tells the Story, Writes History." The chapter opens with information from The Op-Ed Project.[4] The organization's goal is "to increase the number of women thought leaders contributing to commentary forums— which feed all other media, and drive thought leadership across all industries—to a tipping point. They envision a world in which the best ideas---regardless of where or whom they come from — will have a chance to be heard and shape society and the world." Taking the bigger messages and breaking them into voices that can be heard is oursocial media WE.

Finally, one of the most important collaboration opportunities for women to connect with a 10,000 member strong organization is through national certification with the Women Business Enterprise National Council (WBENC).[5] They understand the importance of "Join forces. Succeed together." The president of the organization, Pamela Prince-Eason, comes from a large corporate background and leverages her background wisely as she promotes the importance of being committed to collaboration. She says, "Collaboration will result in progress on the Road to Growth and Sustainability fueling our nation's economy and creating jobs." WBENC's core values — certification, oppportunities, resources and engagement — exemplify all they do. Corporations like Accenture believe strongly in the development of their suppliers with a directed focus on collaboration. They believe collaboration helps to foster growth and lead all toward success. They are very involved with WBENC's mission of helping women succeed.[6]

Below is a self-assessment checklist[7] that can keep you on track if you decide to collaborate. Leaders need to consider this type of framework. A framework example includes the following:

1. **Outcomes and Accountability:** Have short-term and long-term outcomes been clearly defined? Is there a way to track and monitor progress?

2. **Bridging Organizational Cultures:** What are the missions and organizational cultures of the participating team? Has the team agreed on common terminology and definitions?

3. **Leadership:** How will leadership be sustained over the long-term? If leadership is shared, have roles and responsibilities been clearly identified and agreed upon?

4. **Clarity of Roles and Responsibilities**: Have participating teams clarified roles and responsibilities?

5. **Participants:** Have all relevant participants been included? Do they have the ability to commit resources for their agency?

6. **Resources:** How will the collaborative mechanism be funded and staffed? Have online collaboration tools been developed?

7. **Written Guidance and Agreements:** If appropriate, have participating teams documented their agreement regarding how

they will be collaborating? Have they developed ways to continually update and monitor these agreements?

WE transform our lives by collaboration and WE sustain by caring for our people, natural resources and how we dispose of what we use. Working together for the good of all is really a way to streamline processes and allow teams and programs to achieve results. Be encouraged and find a way to collaborate. It will sustain your business and life with insight and best ideas developed and shared by others. Collaboration + Sustainability = Performance for economic and social success.

Footnotes:

1. http://crgsustainablesolutions.com

2. http://businessovercoffee.com

3. http://socialmediainfluence.com/2010/11/16/the-social-media-sustainability-index/

4. http://www.theopedproject.org/

5. http://www.wbenc.org/

6. Al Williams, Chief Procurement Officer, Accenture, 2013 WBENC Summitt and Salute

7. http://www.govexec.com/excellence/promising-practices/2012/10/7-things-you-need-cross- agency-collaboration/58988/

DEBRA NORWOOD

Attorney at Law, Norwood & Atchley

Known as the "LAUGHTER Lawyer USA," Debra is an advocate of unorthodox methods of conflict resolution. She has developed a model for resilience training, anger management and peacemaking that is out of the box yet grounded in sound empirical evidence. She's paid her dues living in the grim mindset that one has to be serious to be effective.

Certified Laughter Lawyer USA advocates laughter, positive psychology and conflict management with a smile so that stressed professionals can become harbingers of peace by Reframing Thinking, Reforming Bad Habits, and Restructuring Public Image. Together we can develop the skills to be cheerful agents for hope in any setting.

Her workshops "Look Good! Feel Good!" show participants how to improve their self-esteem and public presentation through self-regulating strategies which help the inner you and the outward you match. What good is a smile when your heart is breaking? In addition, Debra takes her teambuilding strategies to corporations and organizations ready to transition to the next level by instituting practical strategies to align core values with corporate thinking.

You can find Debra on radio shows: Look Good! Feel Good!,

Your True Colours Image Radio and Bilingual programming: Mi Vida! (My Life), airing on BOCI Talk RadioChannel.

Visit:www.laughterlawyerusa.com

CHAPTER 7

MAKE THE MAGIC HAPPEN
By Debra Norwood

When I think of the word collaboration, my mind goes directly to the people in my life who best represent the principles of networking, cooperation and synergy. These are people who, when given a task, seem to magically "make things happen" by calling upon talents, resources and people as if they were seamlessly fitted to the challenge at hand like a glove fitted for a prize fighter.

I think of one of the master networkers himself, my brother, Milton Chaves, who rose up the ranks from a textbook salesman to the Commercial Section of the American Embassy in Venezuela,ultimately earning the position as a government liaison officer for a major petroleum company.

As an executive in the oil industry, my brother has been called upon to fly into a foreign country at a moment's notice to contact local government officials and stave off an emergency. I have seen the company send him to airports halfway around the world, even diverting him to distant airports to protect him from storms in one continent simply to fly him to a nearer airport in the next, just so he may quickly reach the person who will direct him to the desk of a cabinet minister, or the president of a third world country.

I have seen him open doors in high places and win the hearts of those with whom he has to work, even if he has never met them, all because he has gained the reputation of being single-minded, relentless in purpose, yet authentic and trustworthy in his delivery of information. His rolodex of contacts includes multi-millionaires, chiefs of state, and a "Who's Who" list of important people that would be worth a fortune for the goodwill he has established.

A closer examination of that list of VIPS, however, would also reveal that the same list contains the names of every schoolmate he has ever made friends with since elementary school, as well as every gardener, mechanic, maid, janitor and stranger he ever befriended. My brother values people, remembers their anniversaries and birthdates, and, above all, shows a genuine interest in their daily lives. He is much like our father, Domingo Chaves, who built an empire in Latin America from the sales of agricultural machinery with the same intensity and drive, as well as the same basic respect for the inherent value of the common person.

Each influential person I have ever met seems to have similar core values: my business partner and friend, Carolyn Bendall,

President of Fashion Academy, is another master networker who values all people of all walks of life and seems to pull the right person and pair him to the right task like an illusionist pulls a rabbit out of a hat. Carolyn's gift is also that of authenticity, coupled with humility, integrity and the joy of service. When Carolyn networks, her objective is not to use people, but to help them, to honor them, and to serve them. In return, they express their gratitude by assisting her without question if the need arises.

Two other people whose networking abilities I value are Ivette Baldezon, current Director of Multi-Cultural Affairs for the Shelby County (Tennessee) Mayor, and Isha Echols of UltraCulture—a master storyteller, educator and community activist. I have known both women for nearly 30 years, and can honestly say that their gifts and virtues have remained unchanged and incorruptible throughout the years.

Ivette's gifts of discretion and diplomacy are energized by a fierce commitment to social justice that has served her well. She has become an effective liaison for the Hispanic community and now for the diverse ethnic groups found not only in Shelby County, but also around the Mid-South. Ivette's tireless commitment to do what is right has earned her respect from major corporations, two mayors' offices and local law enforcement as well as the hearts and minds of the immigrants and naturalized citizens she helps on a daily basis. No task is too humble for her—my friend will dedicate herself to helping a mother receive diapers for her children with the same intensity that she dedicates to drafting and advocating a voting ordinance before the city council or a countywide referendum. Furthermore, people know that fact about her—she is committed. In return, they show respect for her dedication and cooperate with her when she needs them, out of loyalty and honor to her.

Isha Echols is another person who works daily, and by choice, prefers to emphasize the one-on-one with individuals, mostly children and "elders," as she calls them, but another of her true gifts is her ability to discern the political climate of an organization. Among her many skills, she is a community garden/ecologist/sustainable living promoter and is experienced in community activism, grant writing and social vision. Isha is a master at supervising others and directing others to find answers within themselves for the challenges they face—she helps empower the weak by encouraging self-sufficiency.In return, she too seems to have that amazing ability to draw upon her army of contacts to mobilize for a cause. It is through Isha that I have come to see a noble example of collaborative community building found in Reno,

Nevada: Conscious Community and Connecting the Good, created by visionary Richard Flyer.

The *Connecting the Good* website is a model of community empowerment, collaboration and advanced core values which foment cooperation, networking and results-oriented activism. Like the principles that drive people I admire, this is an organization that happily lists its values and exhorts its members to embrace them to reach a higher spiritual consciousness. These values cement collaboration, spirituality and excellence of character. I think of these principles as a sort of "Prime Directive," not unlike the one envisioned in the Utopian world of the popular science fiction movies and T.V. series, Star Trek. Contrast these to the feeble and often token corporate "Mission Statements" which are all too oftenused after the fact to justify company actions rather than the other way around.

This organization unabashedly claims that Love, Integrity, Courage, Service, and Respect are the fundamental pillars for an effective society. Below is a direct reproduction of the Community Principles and Virtues as written by Richard Flyer:

WHAT WE STAND FOR

We all share a belief that virtues are important, but they may not be in the forefront of how we live our lives. Conscious Community encourages us to "walk our talk" because we believe that the foundation to a sustainable society is in virtuous behavior towards ourselves and others, generating strong families, tight-knit neighborhoods, communities, and eventually the world.

This list was the result of input from the community and from looking at the "core values" of many social institutions, including service groups such as Rotary, business, the U.S. military and police departments, non-profit and civic organizations, religious groups, city governments, and more.

Love: Power that connects.

- Compassion, Humility
- Kindness, Patience
- Generosity, Joy
- Forgiveness, Appreciation

    Faith, Surrender
- Empathy, Hope

Integrity: Do what is right, the ability to hold together and properly regulate all of the elements of your personality.

- Wisdom, Authenticity

- Responsibility, Self-Reliance

- Honesty, Honor

- Trustworthiness, Simplicity

- Balance

Courage: Strength to do what is right, face your fears, adhere to a higher standard no matter what happens.

- Strength, Self-Discipline

- Perseverance, Self-Restraint

- Acceptance, Openness to others

- Dedication, Nobility

Service: Finding your life purpose, an ethic of "Service to Humanity and all life" each moment.

- Goodwill, Involvement

- Sharing, Community

- Caring Service

Respect: Demonstrating positive regard for yourself and others.

- Mindfulness, Cooperation

  Fairness, Dignity
- Civility, Self-Reflection

  Justice

(Reprinted with permission from www.consciouscommunity-reno.org)

Last but not least, I'd like to speak of the newest networking mentor I met recently through my partner, Carolyn Bendall, and that is Sherri Henley, founder and CEO of Business Over Coffee International (BOCI). Like those I have mentioned before, Sherri also has the ability to find value in everyone she meets, and like Carolyn, is always of service. Like Yvette and Isha, Sherri focuses on organizational systems as well as people. Sherri also helps many discover hidden talents and resources through her mentoring, either through "Professional Boost" programs that she has used to sculpture budding entrepreneurs or by her powerful executive coaching advice and education through the use of formats designed by her; one example is online courses on the use of Social Media as a Networking Tool. Above all, I believe Sherri's talent in "Bringing Everyone Together" at BOCI is grounded in gifts innately found within her of Generosity, Acceptance and Perseverance.

I am thankful for my involvement with Sherri, her

husband and her family, as well as BOCI, not only because of the wonderful things I am learning daily about Social Media Intelligence, but also because of the service that BOCI has provided my company and me personally as Laughter Lawyer USA. By showcasing my business through BOCI Talk Radio and BOCI TV, and by linking me to Virginia Rowland, manager of Ridgeway Business Center, I received my first major media coverage as Laughter Lawyer USA in the *Commercial Appeal,* a Mid-South newspaper. I have learned how to host my own radio show, and have had hundreds of opportunities to present myself on BOCI TV, Video Conferencing, and in face-to-face networking campaigns. In April of 2013, BOCI generously became the major corporate sponsor for Tennessee National Humor Month, which in essence launched me as the Director for National Humor Month, a position that very few certified laughter leaders get to enjoy because of the prohibitive costs of advertising. As a result of BOCI bearing the brunt of the advertising, Tennessee became a top state celebrating month long activities honoring the World Laughter Tour's Good Hearted Living Principles. As a result, psychologist Steve Wilson, the Director of National Humor Month and CEO of World Laughter Tour, participated in our statewide and international celebrations.

I know the lessons we are sharing with others in our virtual and face-to-face events at BOCI all promote the benefits of collaboration –and thus are also indirectly teaching professional members of BOCI the value of sharing, serving and eschewing jealousies and rivalries that often cripple networking. Not everyone is ready to give up on individuality, greed and self-absorption. But the lesson I have learned from the creative mentors in networking that I have listed above — Milton, Carolyn, Ivette, Isha and Sherri — is that they are confident they can mobilize an army to meet a challenge because they never underestimate the value of simple acts of service to others without manipulation. By faithfully conducting themselves with virtue, these networkers have achieved the desired result of developing a vast alliance based on trust, fidelity, loyalty and unity in purpose. Because of Sherri Henley's generosity towards me at BOCI, I now have the opportunity to be recognized as a mover and shaker in my field, and I have the obligation to pay it forward and "make the magic happen" when called upon to do so. This debt to one another is not a bribe for past services, but a moral obligation to spread the wealth by helping people unite for a common cause and ultimately for the purpose of helping one another succeed, resulting in the betterment of all.

I believe this is just the beginning of many more amazing events to come which will impact many BOCI professional members and inspire them to strive for higher standards of service, collaboration, integrity and trustworthiness that Sherri Henley brings to her company. With those core values at the helm, I know my time as an executive committee member at BOCI will someday be remembered as some of the most fruitful, productive, profitable and fun filled days of my life.

TERRI MURPHY

President, Terri Murphy Communications, Inc.

Have you ever wondered how to cut through the chatter to connect with prospects and make real profits? Specializing in communication strategies that build relationships with clients and customers, Terri understands the unmatchable power of **connection** to create more sales in today's competitive marketplace.

Terri is the president of Terri Murphy Communications, Inc. As a consultant and speaker, Terri helps to create new relationships using cutting-edge and traditional marketing and online communication strategies.

She is a published author of five books, including her most recent book with Donald Trump, *The Best Real Estate Advice I Ever Received,* and has authored four additional books on sales and leadership.

Terri is currently writing a book that addresses how women can improve their selection of a relationship by using a little science in the process. She is co-authoring this book with Dr. Paul Green, an industrial psychologist and an expert in behavioral interviewing.

Terri has produced and hosted both television and radio programs, and has been featured on ABC, NBC and CNBC News as a sales industry expert. She is also a regular guest on WREGTV's Live@9 for Women in Business.

Visit: www.WomensWisdomNetwork.com, www.TerriMurphy.com

CHAPTER 8

CONNECT, COMMUNICATE& COLLABORATE
Harnessing the Power of Connection through Communication
By Terri Murphy

Communication is the key to human connection. In business today, whether you are buying, selling, referring, or prospecting, some kind of connection is required. In today's marketplace, there are powerful channels that allow us to connect with virtually anyone on earth, and target very SPECIFIC connections with people who need our services and leverage the services of others....effortlessly!

This new marketplace is noisy, crowded and global in scope, however, so connecting can be a new challenge.

Connecting has gone beyond a simple phone call, fax or letter, and is easier than ever using the Internet. The messaging channels may have changed, but the power of conversation still reigns supreme for us to connect to and work with anyone, anywhere.Use these new channels to attract, connect and engage business. When used effectively, these channels propel you and your business from *invisible* to *incredible* in a surprisingly short period of time!

There are multiple ways to design your online digital footprint, but in this brief chapter, we will help you with the basics of each of the powerhouse channels to launch your global positioning and meet more people, to do more business and to build a community of raving fans.

Google

You are who Google says you are! There are countless factors that will drive you to the first page. Video (YouTube) ranks first, followed by a carefully orchestrated convergence of professional profiles. LinkedIn is where the real power of collaboration takes place, then Facebook and Twitter. Combine these channels with highly targeted information and resources, followed by relevant content on your blog, and you are well positioned for a prime spot on a Google search.

Run a Google search on yourself and see where you come up.If you aren't on the first page of Google, you are, for the most part, invisible. This step is a basic, but critically important one! To be collaborative with businesses and services that need you, you must be found quickly!

Quick Tip: Monitor your online reputation by plugging your name, company and maybe your competition into a Google alert to manage both positive and negative sentiment (posts) so you know what is being said about you.

Linked **in** .

The million dollar network that epitomizes collaboration for business to business contacts is owned by www.LinkedIn.com. LinkedIn is NOT a simple referral network, although it does a spectacular job of networking with other like-minded professionals. The basic power of LinkedIn is the critical psychology of influence, or implied endorsement. When you get endorsed by or are connected to a person of influence, stature, or position, you are automatically viewed in a similar light. This is often referred to as social currency, which is a key reason NOT to just link up with anyone who asks. You areopening your address book, so choose carefully. More importantly, LinkedIn allows for global collaboration through groups and conversational threads that help you with introductions and recommendations that connect and convert conversations to profitability.

1) Provide a professional photo. Avoid using a casual photo unless that is your line of work.

2) Search for people you know on LinkedIn and send a request to be connected. Add a personalization to the default message to provide relevance and a reason to connect with you.

3) Set a goal to give and get testimonials. Give at least one testimonial a week for people you know and have done business with. Remember, you are leveraging your good name on theirs, so be sure this person will deliver what you say they will to protect your good name and reputation.

4) Check your LinkedIn profile at least once or more per week to see who has sent you requests, and determine if they are a good fit for your profile.

facebook

Like other online channels, Facebook is a conversation, and that conversation is the key to getting people to know, like and trust you, one of the key components of relationship selling. Here are some quick tips for developing a digital presence on Facebook:

1) Develop a custom Facebook Business Page with a URL that reflects what you do or your target market. If your name is impossibly long, hard to spell or easily confused with other similar names, think toward a pointer domain that identifies what you do. Example: There are a zillion Terri Murphys out there. If I were

selling cupcakes, I might buy the domain "MemphisCupcakeExpert" to make it easy for people to find me and drive people to my Facebook page.

2) Instead of posting non-relevant information, lay out a simple 30+ day monthly calendar. Plug in your business events, national events and holidays first. Then plug in relevant events and information about what you do and highlight media events like a radio or TV appearance.

Like LinkedIn, leverage social currency with photos that position you as a resource in your marketplace and your community.

twitter

There is not much you can communicate in fewer than 140 characters! Think of Twitter as a simple news feed, or link bait to direct a viewer to your blog or website for more information. Use Twitter as a search for collaborative community interests and commentary that supports your expertise. Local searches are referred to as "Twello" for more local identification.

1) Sign up for Twitter and remember your username and password.

2) Choose your Twitter address to correspond with who you are, what you do and your target market, like@MemphisCupcakes (example).

3) Use a program like HootSuite or DLVR to post on other online channels simultaneously.

4) Post consistently.

5) Avoid messaging with hash tags that don't provide relevance to a viewer's personal interest.

6) Shorten long URLs to fit Twitter by using www.Bit.ly.

You Tube
Broadcast Yourself

Did you know that YouTube has more than 1 billion unique users each month and that over 4 billion hours of video are watched each month online? Google reports that 72 hours of video are uploaded to YouTube every minute, and if you are in business today, some of those uploads should be yours!

One of the top five most searched terms on YouTube is "how-to," giving every entrepreneur a window to platform how or why his services are paramount to a full vital digital online presence.

Here are a few short tips:

1) Credibility rockets when you have your own YouTube Channel. Under that channel, identify "playlists" to help viewers and search engines find what they are looking for fast. Think of introduction, meet the staff, testimonials, educational video clips and media as a good start to filling out your YouTube.

2) Buy a good video camera that has an exterior microphone. This will help you to record good audio. Invest in a tripod, an exterior lavalier microphone and perhaps a hand-held microphone when doing interviews.

3) Set up a video production schedule. Figure out what you want to say, who you want to see your video, and how you want to be positioned. Interview strategic

partners and experts that collaborate in your market space.

4) Always add a call to action at the end of each video.

5) Keep your videos under 2-3 minutes at the most, unless you are making a specific educational video.

6) Check out www.EasyWebVideo.com for a great resource for your videos without those annoying ads, and more.

These tools can only work when you work with them! Think of these channels as exceptional ways to easily connect with specific people and groups, uniquely positioned to collaborate and support what you do and for whom you do it. Communication is the key to connection, and collaboration immediately follows. Connect, Communicate, Collaborate...we all win!

DELMAR JOHNSON, MA

Founder and CEO, Delmar Johnson Enterprises

HR Consultant, Career Coach, Speaker, Author

With over 10 years of experience working with large corporations, small business owners and launching entrepreneurs, human resource guru and visionary Delmar Johnson founded HR Brain for Hire as a trusted and resourceful solution for first time employers in need of affordable, efficient, and top notch recruitment, training and HR services. Delmar's personal story, which includes multiple layoffs, life challenges, and her own dive into entrepreneurship, gives her a perfect mix of formal knowledge and real life experience that she pours into each client and their unique needs. Business owners love Delmar because her talent and passion for HR allow them to fall in love with their business all over again by providing them the right support they so desperately need while saving them time, money, and headaches. Delmar also has an unconditional passion for women in career transition and enjoys sharing her time and knowledge with organizations, non-profit groups and individuals who simply desire a little guidance and a plan during their career preparedness.

Delmar has been featured in *Working Mother Magazine, The Business 101 Magazine* and is a regular contributor to *The Business 101 Magazine*and*The Little Pink Book* online magazine.She is also a contributor to the Women for Hire advice forum, was a career expert for the 2012 Women for Hire online job fair, was highlighted in the NY Daily News.com, Monster.com, and mentioned in the *Women's Elevation Magazine*. Delmar was also selected as a speaker and panelist for the 2011 & 2012 Design Your Destiny Conference, Reinvention Revolution, and has been a featured guest on several Blog Talk Radio shows.

Byoffering solutions, interactive workshops, and training presentations, Delmar's goal is two-fold: 1) To offer value-added solutions to women-owned businesses, positioning them as an ***employer of choice***by establishing HR tools, standards and systems; 2) To equip women to design their own career path by matching up what is in them to what they do.

Visit: www.delmarjohnson.com, www.hrbrainforhire.com

CHAPTER 9

5 KEYS TO BUILDING COLLABORATION THAT WORKS

By Delmar Johnson

It is often said that two heads are better than one; the key is not that it is *just* two heads, but that they are the right ones. The same goes with developing value enriched business collaborations. The best collaborations are usually those where both parties are clear and focused on similar or complimentary businesses, projects or services, increasing the probability of a win-win result.

I have experienced both good and bad collaborations. Here, I offer a perspective of a very recent collaboration gone right, but first I have a few points to share that will be applicable as you pursue your own collaborative partnerships. Five key points should be addressed when deciding to connect with others in a collaborative partnership:

1. **Be clear about your *why*.** Give sincere thought as to why you want to bring someone in on your idea for a service or product. Is it to expand your brand? To develop a platform that adds value to individuals,

groups, or organizations? Is your *why* to have access to an audience you have yet to penetrate? It is imperative that all parties know why the collaboration makes sense and, in knowing that, establish an agreement of what and how things will be accomplished.

2. **Identify each other's strengths and weaknesses.** No two people have the same skill sets, talents or knowledge capacities. Identifying strengths and weaknesses on the front end of a conversation establishes where to delegate certain tasks and responsibilities to achievethe common goals and objectives of the collaborative project.

3. **Be completely honest.** Lies resolve nothing and will ruin everything. Truth in every step and every action is the foundation of a successful collaboration. If there are any questions to be answered of your collaborative partner, ask them immediately and resolve anything that is unclear prior to moving to the next step. In business, people do business with people they know, like and trust. It is the same in collaborative partnerships. There is no fun in working with people who choose to withhold the truth.

4. **Constructively resolve conflicts.** Resolving conflicts quickly increases the opportunity to reach a solution that keeps you focused on meeting previously established goals. As with any team effort, conflicts can and will arise. The worst thing you can do is remain stuck in that conflict. Unresolved conflict breeds resentment, stress and broken agreements, a combination that impedes growth for future accomplishments.

5. **Create timelines for each project.** Timelines create a platform for accountability. Timelines that are well thought out and written down or digitally stored online (in the cloud) in a central location keep everyone on track. Twenty-First Century technology has made this task as easy as 1-2-3. Everything today is in the Cloud, e.g., Google Drive. Project timelines, action steps, revisions, and so much more can be established on a cloud platform, creating the opportunity to see what each party is doing to obtain a common goal.

A Collaboration Gone Right!

In an entrepreneur's journey, there comes a time where risks are to be taken and expected. Going outside the norm and doing things you have never done or doing things that are uncomfortable should become commonplace. Collaborations are the perfect training ground to exercise risks, step out of your comfort zone, and hopefully experience the height of success simultaneously.

The Making of an Event Using Collaboration

It all began in a private coaching session where ideas were discussed and strategies established to build businesses brick by brick. One of the challenges presented to me was to create an event that would serve not only as an opportunity for women in the community to connect, share and learn, but also as strategy to establish my own business brand. As exciting as the idea was, it was also frightening, not just because it was the first time I had done anything
like this, but also because I faced the potential of being overwhelmed by all the moving parts involved in creating a successful event. After a lot of overthinking and procrastination, I finally put a checklist and projected budget together to keep me on track. Neither was followed down to the letter; however, both served as a guide for the next steps.

I asked myself, "How will I pull this off with a very limited to nonexistent budget?" The key was tapping into my network circle and asking for help. First, I needed to find a venue I could use for free or for a minimal amount of money; as a result of my relationship with some awesome people at the National College of Business and Technology Memphis campus, I was able to secure their brand new facility for my first live event, Living In The N.O.W. Women's Summit 2013. Immediately, I felt released from the burden of finding an appropriate facility that was modern, tech savvy and comfortable for the women in attendance.

Next, I embarked upon the search for speakers that could bring value to an audience of dynamic women.Rounding up everyone and getting them on the same page was not the easiest thing in the world to do, but I saw it as something that came with the territory of producing an event that had the potential to grow into something far reaching. It is important to remember that collaboration is all about relationships, in addition to having common interests in what you are striving to achieve.

Third, I needed to reach out and contact entrepreneurs and small business owners in my circle that would consider investing in the event as sponsors and/or vendors. Taking those risks waschallenging, but I kept in mind that it would all be worth it in the end.

People you have built relationships with over time genuinely want to see you succeed and will cheer you on by supporting in a variety of ways, even when they are unable to invest financially. Others' encouragement and assistance in building an event of value, power, and substance is exactly what the bigger picture is all about.

Once I got past my third step I realized that there were many more moving parts in creating and launching the Women's Summit with more collaborative connections to achieve. For example, holes to be plugged were in the areas of event photography, catering, volunteers, promotional materials and entertainment...to name a few. My attitude check was, "No, not an easy task, but it can—and will--be done, made possible by the joint effort of the team I have built."

Success cannot be achieved in a box, *alone*. Sure, we can get many things done by ourselves, but is that really how growth-oriented and forward-thinking entrepreneurs and businesses operate? The answer is NO. Go forth and begin to make a conscious choice to build relationships that morph into unstoppable collaborations.

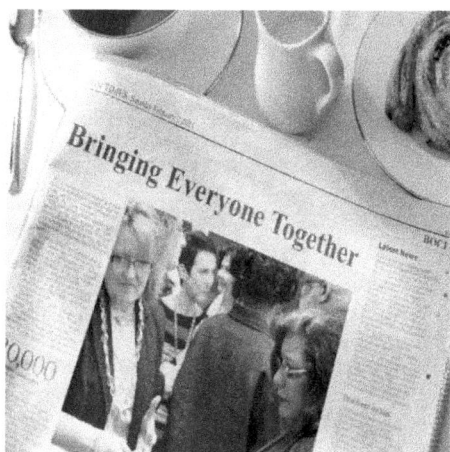

*"There is strength in numbers. **Bringing everyone together** for the purpose of connecting, collaborating and exposure will enlarge the territory of each person in a united circle of influence."* - Sherri Henley

CHAPTER 10

BUILD YOUR PLATFORM FOR MORE THAN ONE
By Sherri Henley

Building your platform for more than one is **paramount to your success as a professional collaborator.** *Growing out instead of up is how you make room for someone other than yourself.*

Collaboration is an unselfish act performed to enhance oneself while promoting another from the same pulpit using different microphones. Take a choir, for instance...when one sings, it is called a solo. Two, a duet.Three, a trio. Four, a quartet. A few more, a choral. Several more, a choir. A choir is unified with harmony or in unison, as one voice,yet there are many parts *and* people who make up a whole from ONE platform. If singers did not collaborate in song, we would never know the harmonious sound of chorus. If musicians did not collaborate in rhythm, we would never know the sound of music to our ears or feel like dancing!

Lyrics from the song, "We Are The World"
performed by collaborative artists to bring everyone
together for a common cause says, in part, "We are
the ones who makes a better day so let's start
giving." Bob Burg, co-author of *The Go Giver* expounds upon
"The Law of Giving and Receiving." The description of this
book reveals thoughts behind giving for the fictional
character, Joe. "Joe learns that changing his focus from
getting to giving—putting others' interests first and
continually adding value to their lives—ultimately leads to
unexpected returns."

So the root of collaboration is
giving? Yes! However, to give, we must trust. In order to
trust, we must know. In order to know, we must connect. In
order to connect, we must meet. In order to meet, we must
SHOW UP! This leads us to the personalized "Show Up to Go
Up" slogan I toss around constantly.

Collaboration begins with a connection. To
become an influencer, you must rub shoulders with mentors
who have *been there and done that*...those who have paved
the way before you. It is up to YOU to find and follow people

who lead by example, as they are not going to babysit you. Do you know why? Because they are too busy following *their* chosen leaders who enhanced *their* understanding along the way.

A successful person has a good understanding of what it means to follow as well as lead. A leader is *first* a follower of another who knows more than he or she. Never get so *big for your britches* that you believe you have learned it all...because you will be pegged as a know-it-all...rightfully so! Those who *lean in* to trailblazers climb the path to greatness while making way for those who walk a few steps behind them.

Picture yourself with two outstretched hands: one reaching up to people of influence, the other reaching down to people of promise. You are being promoted to another level while pulling your protégé up a notch. I call it "The Stair Step Mentality." Climbing the ladder of success while preparing another to take the next step...never stopping...always striving to reach higher heights and deeper depths in your evolution of life.

You may say, "I thought this book was about collaboration in business."***When life becomes your business, your business will become your life.***

Let me explain. I used to dread Monday. I hoped God would add a few hours to the weekend so I could enjoy *"life."* It wasn't until I began to live life to its fullest by pursuing my passion — *what I was created to do* — and embracing my God-given purpose of developing others that I truly realized *life is work...and work is life.* If we are doing what we are put on Earth to accomplish, we become more focused on enhancing ourselves *and* others, which leads to the unselfish nature of collaboration in the business of life!

The authors in this book are collaborators in the truest sense of the word. Each has her own niche, while embracing others and creating an extension of power to share with the world and prospective communities.

Now it is your turn to tap into the wealth of knowledge you have gained from authors in this book. Exercise your power in collaboration by asking and answering these questions:

1. **What have I learned that I did not know?**

2. **How will I apply this to my daily life?**

3. **Who are my mentors?**

4. **Who is my protégé?**

5. Who have I connected with recently?

6. What were our common goals?

7. How can we collaborate to make those goals a reality?

8. When will we start our collaboration?

Once you have answered these questions truthfully, *take action.* Be a doer, not just a dreamer. Catch the concept of collaboration. Join hands, link arms, start building your platform for more than one and continue bringing everyone together...growing *out* instead of *up*!

www.ingramcontent.com/pod-product-compliance
Lightning Source LLC
Chambersburg PA
CBHW070941210326
41520CB00021B/7007